"extremely well-written and researched and entertaining. . . this book fills a genuine gap in providing for the first time a biography of Burns that is suitable for younger readers"

Dr Gerard Carruthers
Director, Centre for Robert Burns Studies,
University of Glasgow

Robert Burns, born in 1759 and who died young in 1796, is the national bard of Scotland. His poems and songs are performed and sung the world over to this day. Born into a poor farming family, in today's terms, the young Robbie was a child labourer. He and his brothers and sisters sometimes had barely enough to eat. Yet his father was keen that his sons and daughters read books and had an education.

Later he escaped with his life in a workshop fire, tried unsuccessfully to be a farmer himself and in desperation thought of emigration to Jamaica. His is an inspiring story.

INSPIRATIONS SERIES

Series Editor: Rosemary Goring

An easy-to-read series of books
that introduce people of achievement
whose lives are inspirational.

Other titles in the series:

Bob Dylan
Nelson Mandela
The Williams Sisters

Further titles to follow in 2011

Robert Burns

Bard of Scotland

Bronwen Hosie

ARGYLL ✠ PUBLISHING

Argyll Publishing
Glendaruel
Argyll PA22 3AE
Scotland
www.argyllpublishing.com

The author has asserted her moral rights.

**British Library Cataloguing-in-Publication
Data.
A catalogue record for this book is available
from the British Library.**

The publisher acknowledges subsidy from the
Scottish Arts Council towards the publication of
this volume.

ISBN 978 1 906134 53 2

Printing: JF Print Ltd, Somerset

dedicated to my father-in-law,
Robert Russell Hosie who first introduced me
to the genius of the Bard of Scotland;
also thanks to my son Alistair who initially
edited and proofread the book for me

Contents

1. Alloway

IT WAS a wild night in Kyle when Robbie was born. January of that year brought terrible weather with it, more terrible than anyone could ever remember.

Agnes McClure, who was the village midwife, and wife to John Tennant the blacksmith, said she had never seen the like and hinted that it was a sign; a sign that the newborn baby would have a life as wild as the awful weather.

William Burness saw that his wife, Agnes, was looking anxiously at her infant son and told the midwife she was talking nonsense.

'Auld wifies' tales,' he scorned and early next morning, on the 26th, rode into town to fetch the minister for his son's baptism. The weather was still sharp and fresh but the wind had eased.

'What did you name the laddie?' the Session Clerk asked as he wrote down the details in a neat hand in the parish register.

'Robert, after his grandfather,' William Burness replied proudly, and the clerk wrote it down, spelling the surname 'Burns' the Ayrshire way.

The stormy weather continued and some nine or ten days later a part of the gable end of the cottage fell away. It happened just before daylight. Robbie's mother was worried that her baby would be harmed so her husband helped her through the biting storm as they struggled to reach their neighbour's house. They stayed there for a full week before their own place was set to rights again.

William Burness had built the cottage and made a good job of it. His 'clay biggin' he called it. He was upset because the storm had damaged a part of the gable but was pleased that he had been able to repair it.

The cottage had a kitchen at one end, and a room in the other, with a fireplace and a chimney. He had made a hidden bed in the kitchen, with a small closet at the end – both made of the same materials as the cottage – and, when he'd covered all of the walls, outside and inside, with lime, and put a thatched roof on, it had a neat, comfortable appearance.

A door from the kitchen led into the barn and cowshed. There were windows in both rooms, at the front and at the back; but only the one at the front had glass. The other windows had only wooden shutters which could be opened or closed according to the weather. It was a home any decent farming family could be proud of.

William Burness was very pleased that his 'clay biggin' was a good place for his wife and baby son to

RANTIN', ROVIN' ROBIN

There was a lad was born in Kyle,
But whatna day o' whatna style,
I doubt it's hardly worth the while
To be sae nice wi' Robin.

> *Chorus*
> Robin was a rovin' boy,
> Rantin', rovin', rantin', rovin',
> Robin was a rovin' boy,
> Rantin', rovin', Robin!

Our monarch's hindmost year but ane
Was five-and-twenty days begun,
'Twas then a blast o' Janwar' win'
Blew hansel in on Robin.

The gossip keekit in his loof,
Quo' scho: 'Wha lives will see the proof,
This waly boy will be nae coof:
I think we'll ca' him Robin.'

The village of Alloway is in **Kyle**
The **monarch** was George II (1727-1760)
hansel: a good luck gift
keekit in his loof: peeped into the palm of his hand (to foretell his future)
waly: sturdy
coof: a fool

'He'll hae misfortunes great an' sma',
But aye a heart aboon them a',
He'll be a credit till us a' –
We'll a' be proud o' Robin.'

'But sure as three times three mak nine,
I see by ilka score and line,
This chap will dearly like our kin',
So leeze me on thee! Robin.'

---

aboon: above
ilka: every
score and line: refers to the lines on the palm of
his hand
kin': kind, sort,
leeze: approve

live. He had also rented seven acres of ground for a garden, and was sure that he would be able to grow enough fruit and vegetables to sell at the market in Ayr and still have some left over for his family to eat.

In time the vegetable garden proved to be a disappointment. The ground was not much good for growing things so when he was offered a job as head gardener on a nearby estate, Robbie's father decided it would be foolish to turn it down. The estate was owned by Provost Fergusson who was a wealthy retired doctor. His new mansion house had tree-lined avenues and fine laid-out gardens. There were also shrubberies and plantations of trees to be looked after.

As his father worked to the best of his ability for Provost Fergusson, Robbie's mother worked hard on the much smaller piece of land that they now rented. She kept a few cows; enough to produce milk, butter and a few mild cheeses which she sometimes sold at the town market. The poultry she looked after provided eggs and sometimes, for a very special occasion, she would boil one of the oldest hens.

Robbie's mother was used to hard work. Her own mother had died when she was just a young girl of ten. Her father, Gilbert Broun, was always busy on the farm, so after her mother died she had to look after her younger brothers and sisters.

The only chance of schooling that Robbie's mother ever had, along with a few other girls, was at a nearby weaver's cottage. There she had learned to recite the psalms by heart and to do some easy reading. She was never taught arithmetic or how to write; not even her own name.

Her father married again and she was sent to live with her Granny Rainie at a farm in Maybole. There, living with her blind uncle William, and old Granny Rainie, she had spent most of her time indoors spinning; outside she ploughed the land.

The only small pleasure she had was in singing old ballads to her uncle and grandmother as she sat at the spinning wheel. Her uncle loved to hear her singing old Scottish ballads. When she met William Burness on a market day in Maybole she realised that he was a good man who would always be kind to her. She was happy with her husband, William, and proud of the cottage he had built for her.

As Robbie grew up he too was happy at the cottage. Most days he spent with his mother as she worked around the cottage or cared for the animals. She was always cheerful and lively, singing old songs as she worked. Robbie loved it when her dark eyes sparkled and she tossed her head in rhythm as she sang.

Almost as soon as he could walk she taught him how to collect the eggs without breaking them. In the evenings as she again busied herself about the cottage cleaning and cooking, Robbie loved to follow her around listening to more songs.

Four months from Robbie's second birthday, towards the end of September, his brother was born in the cottage. He was named Gilbert after his mother's father. Robbie loved his little brother and as soon as Gilbert could walk he taught him how to carry an egg without breaking it.

When Gilbert was older Robbie showed him how to spin a top, and often the two could be seen trying to catch minnows in the burn near the cottage or trying to race leaf boats and shouting with excitement as the boats floated off towards the River Doon.

Their cottage was quite near a place they called the auld kirk. It had been a ruin for a long time. Part of the roof had caved in; what was left of the roof was covered in a mass of dark vegetation. The branches trailing from the roof to the ground were choked with clinging ivy and full of insects and creatures.

The ivy clambered through the broken windows and wound itself tightly around anything it could get hold of, even causing stones on the floor to rise and become uneven as it forced its roots into the cracks between them.

The first time the boys saw the auld kirk was when their father took them with him. William Burness was sorry to see the building in such a state and grouped together a small work party of villagers to try to tidy up the kirkyard and repair the fallen and broken headstones. There was little that could be done with the kirk itself. William Burness, busy with supervising the clean-up, warned his sons to be careful but Robbie was excited about exploring the spooky ruin. He had heard stories of the auld kirk from his mother's cousin, Betty Davidson, who sometimes lived in the cottage with them. She carried out odd jobs around the garden and cottage for her keep, but in the evenings when it was too dark to work outside and she had settled the cows in the byre for the night she loved nothing better than to sit on a stool by the fire and tell stories.

She was a good storyteller and many an evening she took great pleasure in telling Robbie and Gilbert terrifying tales of strange creatures. Robbie, who was good at learning things off by heart, could list the names of the good and evil characters she spoke of in her stories; ghosts, fairies, brownies, witches, warlocks, spunkies, kelpies, elf-candles, dead lights, wraiths, apparitions, cantraips, enchanted towers, giants, dragons, and all sorts of nonsense. Some of the names he had heard before and some were new to him.

A kelpie, Betty Davidson had explained, is a water spirit. Sometimes he appears in the form of a short, hairy man but usually he is seen as a wild young colt that enjoys throwing its riders into the sea, and sometimes he is half horse and half bull with long sharp horns.

'Best to keep far from a kelpie, laddie!' she advised.

From TAM O' SHANTER*

When, glimmering thro' the groaning trees,
Kirk Alloway seem'd in a bleeze;
Thro' ilka bore the beams were glancing;
And loud resounded mirth and dancing.

Inspiring, bold John Barleycorn!
What dangers thou canst make us scorn!
Wi' tippenny, we fear nae evil;
Wi' usquabae we'll face the devil!
The swats sae ream'd in Tammie's noddle,
Fair play, he car'd nae deils a boddle.
But Maggie stood right sair astonish'd,
Till, by the heel and hand admonish'd,
She ventur'd forward on the light;
And wow! Tam saw an unco sight!

---

* One of Burns most famous poems is set in
the graveyard of Alloway Auld Kirk. Maggie is
the name of Tam's horse.
bleeze: a blaze
ilka bore: every hole, chink
John Barleycorn: a name for whisky or
            beer made from barley
tippenny: twopence beer
usquabae: whisky
boddle: a small coin

Warlocks and witches in a dance;
Nae cotillion brent new frae France,
But hornpipes, jigs, strathspeys, and reels,
Put life and mettle in their heels:
A winnock-bunker in the east,
There sat auld Nick, in shape o' beast;
A towsie tyke, black, grim, and large,
To gie them music was his charge;
He screw'd the pipes and gart them skirl,
Till roof and rafters a' did dirl.

Coffins stood round, like open presses;
That shaw'd the dead in their last dresses;
And by some devilish cantraip slight
Each in its cauld hand held a light
By which heroic Tam was able
To note upon the haly table,
A murderer's banes in gibbet airns,
Twa span-lang, wee, unchristened bairns;

---

cotillion: the name of a dance
winnock bunker: a window seat
tousie tyke: shaggy dog
dirl: vibrate
cantraip: a magic spell, a trick
haly: holy
airns: irons

A thief, new-cutted frae a rape,
Wi' his last gasp his gab did gape;
Five tomahawks, wi' bluid red-rusted;
Five scymitars, wi' murder crusted;
A garter, which a babe had strangled;
A knife, a father's throat had mangled,
Whom his ain son o' life bereft,
The gray hairs yet stack to the heft:
Wi' mair o' horrible and awfu',
Which even to name would be unlawfu'.

rape: rope
gab: mouth
bereft: separated
heft: handle

Robbie felt really sorry for the Spunkies. Betty Davidson said they were ghosts of children who had not been given a name. She said that they wandered the countryside looking for someone to give them a name and they could turn into white moths in order to hide from adults. Robbie was glad that he and his brother Gilbert had been baptised and given names a day after they were born.

So it was, with his head full of such stories, a pounding heart and wide-eyed little Gilbert tailing him, Robbie escaping from the brightness of the day first crept through the shadows of the auld kirk.

At every step he stopped to hold his breath and listen, expecting any moment some ghoulish creature to pounce out of the gloom in front of him, slyly brush him on a shoulder, or sweep his little brother off to some enchanted place in the sky.

Robbie often went back to the auld kirk after that, usually dragging Gilbert along. He was very excited one day on finding some ragwort in the kirkyard because Betty Davidson had told him a story about witches and ragwort. She had told him that dark forces such as witches and warlocks, and even the devil, used the stem of the ragwort as a means of transport.

Robbie kept Betty Davidson's stories to himself; his father always told her she was filling the boys' heads with superstition and nonsense.

2. School Lessons

ROBBIE and Gilbert were soon at an age when their father, concerned about the education of his family, arranged to hire a schoolmaster. He did not have the means to do this himself, but he joined with four other farming families so that together they could afford the services of a young man named John Murdoch.

It was on a windy day in March when William Burness rode to Ayr and arranged to meet the young schoolmaster at a local inn. Having examined carefully how well John Murdoch could write and being pleased with this, William decided he would be fit for the job.

'You'll start in May then, Mr. Murdoch. My four neighbours and I will provide a salary for you and you can board with each one of us in turn.'

John Murdoch, who was born in Ayr and had been educated there and at Edinburgh, arrived in May as arranged and started teaching. Robbie's father liked the young schoolmaster and was pleased with the progress his sons soon made in reading and writing. The school was held in a tenement close to the cottage belonging to Robbie's family. One day, not long after he and his brother had started school, Mr. Murdoch left the classroom for a short while to talk to a visitor. The children thought this a grand excuse to play around and become unruly.

Robbie thought it would be fun to hide in the cupboard near his seat which was close to the classroom door. Everyone called the cupboard a press; it was quite shallow but Robbie, being only six, fitted into it easily.

Mr. Murdoch, on hearing the noise the children were making, came back into the classroom and in order to quieten them slapped the strap he was holding against the door of the cupboard. Robbie, taken by surprise when this happened, screamed out at the amplified thwack and started to cry.

Gilbert could hardly believe that his big brother, who was always so bold in his eyes, could cry so long and hard. Mr. Murdoch did his best to calm Robbie down but he kept crying so much that he was told to go home.

'Robbie whatever is wrong?' his mother asked in concern when he arrived at the cottage still crying. Robbie was still sobbing so pitifully that it took some time before he could answer. 'The master payed me!' he said, meaning 'punished'.

'Payed you, Robbie. What for did the master pay ye? Where did he pay you on?'

'He p-p-payed me on the press!' said poor Robbie.

This caused his mother to laugh out loudly. She had a strap, or tawse as she called it, in the cottage to discipline the children but she hardly ever picked it up to punish them. She was relieved that it was the press that had been strapped and not her son.

Robbie soon learned that school was mostly enjoyable. His schoolmaster taught the pupils as much as possible with the few books he had. Some schools of the same sort had practically no books other than the Bible and most homes already had one of their own. Robbie's father used to read verses out loud from his Bible every evening to his boys.

The school was really no more than a room. There were a few stools but the children usually sat on the floor to listen to the schoolmaster and tried to remember what he read to them.

John Murdoch soon realised that Robbie was quick to learn but could sometimes show signs of stubbornness for which he was occasionally thrashed. The schoolmaster thought that little Gilbert, on the other hand, who was quick with his answers and not as serious as Robbie, seemed to show more promise. Robbie especially loved reading and spent every spare minute he had at the cottage with his nose in a book – not that he had much spare time, as he had to rise early every morning before school to help his mother or father and after school there were always more jobs to be done. Sometimes the reading he was given at school by Mr. Murdoch seemed far too difficult for a boy of his age but his schoolmaster always explained carefully the meaning of each word and made sure that Robbie understood what he was reading.

A story that became a favourite with him from one of his school books was called *The Visions of Mirza*, which was written by a man called Joseph Addison. It was a very difficult story for children to understand but Robbie was very clever and could even learn long poems and passages off by heart.

The story told of a man called Mirza who lived in the Orient. Robbie really enjoyed this story; he loved the scenery that was described in it and the magical adventure.

'I am sure that you will never forget the meanings now,' Mr. Murdoch had said, 'as you are an excellent scholar of English, 'though your musical ear and your brother's,' he added, 'still leave much to be desired.' Robbie took no heed of what Mr. Murdoch said about his singing; all he knew was that he loved tunes and could sing them all perfectly in his head.

His reading became so good that soon he could read books on his own. Many an evening, while his father and John Murdoch discussed religion or a book that his father was reading, Robbie would sit at the table as near to the candlelight as possible to read new stories.

One was the story of Hannibal which Mr. Murdoch

had loaned him. Hannibal was a general who fought against the Romans. The part of the story Robbie liked best was when Hannibal crossed the Pyrenees with an army of 50,000 infantry, 9,000 cavalry and 37 elephants; and then crossed a river, ferrying his elephants across the water on large rafts. Robbie thought Hannibal must have been a great general to think of such things.

Robbie loved playing at 'sodgers' and when the recruiting band sometimes came to the town of Ayr on market day with its drum and bagpipes to try to persuade young men to join the army, Robbie, with great delight, would march behind the band wishing he was tall enough to be a soldier.

Robert Burns

3. Mount Oliphant

WILLIAM Burness was worried. He knew that when Robbie reached the age of eight or nine it was almost certain that his son would have to be hired out as a labourer at a neighbouring farm, as was the custom. Even worse than this was the thought that Robbie might have to be sent off to a farm much further away to work and no longer be able to live at home with his family. William Burness did not want this for his son.

Robbie and Gilbert were no longer the only children; they now had two sisters, little Agnes who was three and baby Annabella. William Burness wanted Robbie, and all of his children, to be educated and have a chance to make a future for themselves. So it was that when Robbie was six and Gilbert had just turned four his father decided to rent a farm of his own. At this time his employer, Provost Fergusson, had recently bought a farm called Mount Oliphant; William Burness asked if he could lease the farm. This meant that although he would not own it, he would be able to work the farm and live in it as a tenant.

Provost Fergusson agreed to let his gardener take over the running of the farm. William Burness was greatly relieved as the cottage at Alloway had become a bit cramped and the farm house, he thought, would provide more room. But mostly he was relieved because he would be able to keep Robbie with the family.

Although the lease started in November, the family was not able to move in until the following May, after Whitsun. The farm was roughly two miles further south from the cottage at Alloway.

Robbie and Gilbert were really excited at moving to a better and bigger home but they were disappointed when they saw that the farmhouse was not a great deal bigger than the 'clay biggin' in Alloway.

It had two rooms; a room and a kitchen which they called the 'but' and the 'ben' on either side of the doorway. There was one window in the 'but' and one window in the 'ben'. It was built of stone, as were the outbuildings, and had a slate roof which they found strange after the thatched roof of the 'clay biggin'.

Robbie and Gilbert slept in the attic, which had no windows at all and was very dark. At night Robbie used to lie awake listening to the sound of rats scurrying in the darkness.

The weather was good that season and they had some time to explore their new surroundings. But they did not have much free time. They still had to rise early every morning to help with the farm work. After a quick breakfast of porridge the boys had to set out on the two-mile walk to school and make sure they did not arrive late as they feared the tawse.

Going to school was downhill and they often half walked and half ran their way; returning home was more of a task – uphill all the way and more work to do as soon as they reached the farm.

Mount Oliphant was remote. At the cottage Robbie and Gilbert had been used to playing with other boys after school, or chatting to neighbours or passers-by. At their new home there were no near neighbours, no passers-by and no other children to play with. They rarely saw anybody other than the members of their own family. Their new home sat with its back to the strong westerly winds, the outbuildings running either side of it to form a yard at the front. Robbie sometimes sat at the highest point he could find to gaze at the changing moods of the Firth of Clyde and the occasional ships passing by.

Often he would watch the soaring and diving of gannets in the air and follow them with his eyes as they made their way across the Firth to their home and their colony on the nearby rock of Ailsa Craig.

Robbie's mother had told him that their feathers were collected from the island and used to make soft mattresses. He decided that he would have a bed made from gannet feathers when he was a man.

In the evenings Robbie loved to sit close to the fire and listen as his mother sang old Scottish songs or told them stories she had learned from her mother.

Sometimes, he was so tired from the work on the farm it was all he could do to keep his eyes open long enough to hear everything; especially when it seemed every bone in his body was aching and his head thumping from the strain of so much hard labour.

Robbie's work was no longer the easy task of collecting eggs. He and Gilbert had to fetch water from the spring, clean out the byres, tend to the horses and accompany their father when he was ploughing to move stubborn rocks out of the way of the plough. When he was sowing the seed they had to scare off the small birds, crows and gulls by shouting at them and waving their arms in the air.

So it was that when Robbie seemed so fatigued, his mother, gently shaking him, would tell him to go to bed. He often drifted into an uneasy sleep in the blackness of the attic and it was only gradually that the sound of rats and the smell of the animals below faded away.

When Robbie was eight and a half his mother gave birth to another baby. Robbie and Gilbert had been named after their grandfathers, as was the custom; the new baby took the name of his father, William.

The boys were pleased with their new little brother but now it meant they had even more tasks to do as their mother, nursing the baby, needed as much help as they could manage. Robbie and Gilbert found that any spare time they used to have was now spent in

quería

keeping their sisters out of mischief. Agnes was five and quite a sensible lass but Annabella, still only three, could get into all kinds of scrapes.

The farm had seventy acres of land, ten times as big as the vegetable garden at the small cottage in Alloway where Robbie had been born. But the soil at Mount Oliphant was not good for planting. It was poorly drained and many a day Robbie and Gilbert watched helplessly as their father struggled to push the plough through water-logged clumps of earth.

Despite his problems, William Burness talked to his sons as they worked together, speaking to them as if they were men and trying to discuss subjects that would increase their knowledge or enlarge upon how they should live a good life.

When Robbie was nine his schoolmaster decided to take on a new teaching post in Dumfries, which was a good distance away.

Shortly before he was due to leave, John Murdoch visited Mount Oliphant with gifts for the family to remember him by. One was a small book of English grammar and the other was a play, the tragedy *Titus Andronicus* by William Shakespeare.

Robbie and Gilbert raced through their work that afternoon to make sure everything was done as John Murdoch had promised to read some of the play to them that evening.

As the darkness fell outside, so the family gathered

around the table inside the farmhouse, William Burness, his wife Agnes, Robbie and Gilbert. Young Agnes, Annabella and baby William were already in their bed. John Murdoch, sitting close to the candle-light, opened the book and started to read out loud.

Everyone listened carefully in order to follow the story and not miss a thing. The play told of the death of an Emperor of Rome, and of his two sons squabbling about which one of them was to become the new leader. Neither of them was chosen as the people wanted Titus Andronicus, a great general.

John Murdoch read on into the late hours and hardly a breath was heard from his rapt audience as they followed the story. Robbie was on the edge of the seat he was sharing with Gilbert, not because of lack of room but because he was so excited. The story continued with much intrigue and turns of plot until it came to the point in the play when Lavinia, the beautiful daughter of Titus, had her tongue cut out and her hands chopped off.

John Murdoch stopped reading at the sudden gasp of horror around the table and looked up from his book, surprised to see Robbie, Gilbert and their mother in tears.

William Burness wisely pointed out that as the book distressed them so much it would be pointless for Mr. Murdoch to leave them with it.

'If you leave it I shall burn it,' Robbie burst out.

His father, shocked at Robbie's bad manners, was just on the verge of telling him off when John Murdoch broke in.

'The lad's sympathy for the poor Lavinia does him credit. I am pleased to see he has so much sensibility. I have another book I can leave instead and I can promise you it will cause no upset.'

That night, as Robbie and Gilbert lay in the dark listening to the regular breathing of their schoolmaster who had stayed the night and was sleeping on the other side of the attic, they did not fall asleep in case their dreams were filled with poor Lavinia's terrible fate.

As the boys said farewell to John Murdoch early the following morning he promised to keep in touch.

'You will enjoy the other book,' he reminded them as he mounted his horse. He was right, for it was a comedy which the family read later and was a welcome relief from the horror of Shakespeare's tragedy.

The little school at Alloway being closed, Robbie and Gilbert now spent all their time at Mount Oliphant with no opportunity of seeing any of their old school friends.

The year dragged out. William Burness needed his sons to help him with labour during the short daylight hours. There was too much for him to do on his own and he had no means of paying hired labourers. When he had arranged to take over Mount Oliphant he had hoped to raise some money by letting out the 'clay biggin' but the cottage remained empty. His landlord, Provost Fergusson, had great faith in the farm being a success and gave him a loan of £100, which was used to buy animals, equipment and seed.

The buildings also needed some repair so every penny of the loan was used up. On top of the £40 rent each year it was a great sum to pay back but William Burness was not too worried as he believed that the farm would be successful.

During the cold winter evenings he coached his sons in arithmetic. As the brothers huddled together to take advantage of the candlelight, their sisters, aged seven and five, picked up whatever they could understand as they watched the boys at their lessons.

As soon as he could find the time that winter, William Burness borrowed books to teach his sons. He laid out a sum of money to become a member of the library at Ayr and borrowed books about geography, natural history, history and astronomy. Robbie and Gilbert were excited about the books and read whenever they could find a few spare minutes but it was Robbie who loved the books so much that he could hardly wait to finish one book before starting the next.

His father also paid a subscription for a series of books called Stackhouse's 'History of the Bible', which was distributed from Kilmarnock. Robbie learned a great deal about ancient history from these. He was in book heaven; it did not matter to him if the books were old, or smelly, or had hundreds of pages; nothing curbed his enthusiasm.

At night, as he sat in bed in the attic shivering with the cold and trying to read from the dim light of an almost used-up candle, he dreaded the end of the winter when he would have to spend every day working full-time again on the farm.

The next year began with no more promise than the last. Their mother gave birth to another boy who was named John. Their father lost several of his animals through accidents and illness, which was a severe blow. As a result the family had to live as frugally as possible in order to try to replace them.

They hardly ever saw meat on their plates, not even an old boiled chicken, and the family had to make do with porridge, oat cakes and bannocks which their mother made from the unleavened oats. Robbie and Gilbert always felt hungry.

That year they worked hard on the farm, their school days with Mr. Murdoch becoming just a memory. One season led on to another with the same daily trek after their father as he struggled to plough the rough infertile land of the Mount Oliphant farm, the same scattering of the birds, the same threshing of the corn, hot and sweating in the sun, wet and miserable in the rain and chilled to the bone when the cold set in.

Robbie kept dreaming of the short days and long dark winter evenings to come when he would again have time to read the books he cherished so much. November finally arrived, cold and bleak as expected; however so did the terrible news that Provost Fergusson, their father's landlord, had died.

Mount Oliphant now passed into the hands of a factor whose job it was to oversee how William Burness was running the farm and also to collect the rent and any other money that was due. Provost Fergusson had been very patient and understanding if William Burness was late in paying the rent or was really short of money from one month to the next. The factor was not at all patient and was angry if William Burness could not pay on time.

Many threatening and nasty letters arrived at Mount Oliphant demanding immediate payments. William Burness became stressed and anxious at the difficult situation he was in and worried that the factor might throw him and his family out of the farmhouse.

Robbie and Gilbert came to dread the arrival of these letters. Often the boys and their mother were in tears because of the unhappy position they were now in; they were all working as hard as possible to make a success of the farm and still they were poor. Robbie worked so hard that he scarcely had enough strength left at the end of the day to climb the ladder up to the attic. It seemed that nothing they did could ever improve their situation.

By the time Robbie was twelve and his little sister, Isabella, had been born, he was even taking turns at driving the plough while Gilbert helped to thresh the corn. Their father desperately needed their help on the farm and could see no way out either for himself or his sons.

William Burness was saddened that their lives had come to this. He had wanted a comfortable life for his family and had especially wanted his children to receive a good education. It was with great sorrow that he noticed his sons' schooling had seemed to come to a standstill and that neither of them could write as well as he would have wished.

The following summer John Murdoch returned from Dumfries and being, once more, in the area of Mount Oliphant paid the family a visit. He noted how tired the boys were and their father told him how bad he felt because he could not improve their education any further.

'Robbie is getting terrible headaches,' he told him, 'and an awful aching in his joints.'

The two men discussed the problem and from that moment William Burness decided that something would have to be done. So it came about during the summer that Robbie, who was now thirteen and Gilbert who was almost twelve, took it in turns to visit the nearest school to their home, the parish school of Dalrymple. One week Robbie worked on the farm to help his father while Gilbert walked almost three miles to school. The following week it was Gilbert's turn to work on the farm while Robbie, full of joy, would almost skip and run the miles towards the little village.

Dalrymple was made up of a church, the manse which stood a few yards from the church gate and a few adjacent cottages. At the school Robbie made friends with a boy called James McCandlish. James, who was a few months younger than Robbie, was a son of Harry McCandlish the blacksmith. James lived at Purclewan farm, which was on the old Roman road not far from Ayr. Next to Gilbert, he became Robbie's best friend.

Robbie had met the blacksmith before when he and his father took the horses from Mount Oliphant to be shod. The next time Robbie went, he was not so shy, having become a good friend of the black-smith's son.

'Your faither telt me ye ken books weel, Rabbie,' he said. 'Here, I have a book for ye. *The Wallace* by Blin' Harry, the minstrel.'

Robbie was very excited with the loan of another book and hugged it tightly to his chest as they rode home. It was a book containing a very long ballad which told of the adventures of William Wallace, the great defender of Scotland who had beaten the army of the English King Edward I at the Battle of Stirling Bridge.

There were many adventures in this story.

BRUCE TO HIS MEN AT BANNOCKBURN*

Scots, wha hae wi' Wallace bled,
Scots, wham Bruce has aften led;
Welcome to your gory bed,
Or to victorie!

Now's the day, and now's the hour;
See the front o' battle lour:
See approach proud Edward's pow'r –
Chains and slaverie!

---

*The **Battle of Bannockburn** (24th June 1314) was a great Scottish victory in the Wars of Scottish Independence. Robert the Bruce and William Wallace were great heroes of Robert Burns. This song he wrote is considered as Scotland's alternative national anthem.
wha: who
hae: have
Wallace was the great Scottish hero William Wallace (born c1272, died 1305)
wham: whom
Bruce was the Scottish King Robert I who was born in Ayr; he was also known as Robert the Bruce (1274–1324)
gory: bloody
lour: look threatening
Edward was the English King Edward I (1239-1307)

Wha will be a traitor-knave?
Wha can fill a coward's grave?
Wha sae base as be a slave!
Let him turn and flee!

Wha for Scotland's King and Law
Freedom's sword will strongly draw,
Freeman stand, or freeman fa',
Let him follow me!

By oppression's woes and pains!
By your sons in servile chains!
We will drain our dearest veins,
But they shall be free!

Lay the proud usurpers low!
Tyrants fall in every foe!
Liberty's in every blow!
Let us do or die!

---

fa': fall

Unlike Hannibal, who lived in a strange land and a far-off time, the Scottish hero William Wallace had visited the places that Robbie had heard of. Although the great hero who fought the English had been captured and killed some three hundred and fifty years before Robbie was born, his memory still lived on in the Scottish peoples' minds as if it were yesterday. Robbie knew that William Wallace would always be his very special hero.

He read these adventures over and over again and as he helped with the threshing of the corn crop his mind was full of the stories. Robbie just knew that he loved anything to do with his great hero and believed the tales Blind Harry told with all his heart.

The following year John Murdoch remained at Ayr teaching English. He did not forget Robbie's love of books and sent a copy of Alexander Pope's poetry.

Later that year, in the summer, although Robbie had to help with the harvest, he was given three weeks off, one before the harvest and two after, to stay with John Murdoch for more schooling.

He revised English grammar during the first week so that he would be able to teach his brothers and sisters at the farm. The last two weeks he mainly studied French and some Latin. Robbie found that French came easily to him; his schoolmaster was astonished at the quick progress he made in the language and they were both sorry when the time came for Robbie to return to Mount Oliphant.

By the time Robbie reached his fifteenth birthday he could handle a plough as well as any man. His father, now over fifty, relied on Robbie and Gilbert more and more to carry out the work, but it was on Robbie, being the eldest, that the hardest work fell. Gilbert noticed that Robbie's headaches seemed to come more often and his spirits seemed low at times. Sometimes Robbie woke up gasping for breath and Gilbert would rush to his mother for a bowl of lukewarm water which seemed to help his brother's breathing if he put his feet in it.

When summer came again there was no time for more studying but just the constant early rising and long days of work that good weather always brought to farming.

That summer Robbie met Nelly Kilpatrick. His father had hired some extra workers to bring in the harvest and Nelly, the daughter of a blacksmith, was one of them. Robbie and Nelly were put to work together; as he gathered the sheaves it was her job to tie the bundles.

Robbie was used to having girls around as he had three sisters but he was not used to working with any girls near his own age and Nelly was only a year younger than Robbie.

She was a very pretty girl with a lovely smile and it was no wonder that Robbie's heart beat faster when he looked at her. After work was finished in the fields for the day, Robbie liked nothing better than loitering behind so that he could walk along the lanes with Nelly as she made her way home.

He sometimes held her hands in order to pick out the nettle stings and thistles which had pierced her skin as she tied the sheaves. Whenever he did this Robbie felt his pulse racing. He had never known these feelings before and could not understand why he felt this way; all he knew was that he thought Nellie was 'a bonie, sweet, sonsie lassie'.

Nelly liked to sing, which she did in a pleasant voice. Robbie was so taken with Nelly that he wrote words to her favourite tune. It was the first time he had ever written in rhyme.

> 'O, once I lov'd a bonie lass
> Ay, and I love her still
> And whilst that virtue warms my breast,
> I'll love my handsome Nell'.

Robbie thought that he would adore Nelly for ever.

Robert Burns

4. Kirkoswald

WHEN Robbie was seventeen his father sent him to Kirkoswald to study land surveying and mathematics at a school whose master, Hugh Rodger, was well known as a very good teacher.

Kirkoswald was a fair distance from Mount Oliphant and was close to the coast, some four miles south west of Maybole where Robbie's mother had lived with her Granny Rainie.

There was much drunkenness in the village at that time because alcohol, amongst other forbidden things, was being smuggled onto the nearby shore. The miles of beach had hidden inlets and small coves where smugglers sailing from the Isle of Man could bring their goods into land unseen. There were large caves in the rocks and cliffs where the illegal goods could be hidden. Many men, wives and even children from Kirkoswald went down to the beach to trade for smuggled goods; tea or tobacco, silk from France and especially brandy.

Some years before, Robbie's own uncle, Samuel, had been accused of smuggling by the local church elders. What concerned them most was the fact that it had been on a Sunday – the Sabbath. Robbie's uncle had protested that he had been to church that morning; it was only after church that he had strolled down to the shore to watch a ship that had arrived from the Isle of Man.

The year after, forty eight men, mostly farmers and farm tenants, were charged with smuggling, taking ankers of brandy from the Manx ships. Uncle Samuel was one of them.

Robbie stayed with his Uncle Samuel's family at Ballochneil farmhouse which was a mile from the village. Uncle Samuel, Aunt Margaret and their daughter Jenny, who was nine, had a small place to live in just outside the main farmhouse which belonged to Aunt Margaret's father. Robbie slept in the attic of the big house with John Niven, who was Aunt Margaret's brother. John was a grown man of twenty one and told Robbie many stories about Kirkoswald and the smugglers.

Although excited at being so far from home, and delighted at the adventure of having smugglers in the district, Robbie was determined to study well. He knew his father must have struggled to save enough money to pay for the schooling. At first he worked really hard at school and for weeks made good progress.

He became friendly with many boys at the school. Thomas Orr was one of them. He lived on a farm called Laigh Park. Robbie had heard from John Niven that Thomas had a grandmother who had much to do with buying goods from the smugglers. Someone at school had told him something that was even worse; she was thought to be a witch.

Willie Niven, who was boarding at the school through the week, became another of his new friends. Willie's father was a brother of Aunt Margaret's father, which made Willie and Aunt Margaret cousins. Robbie felt that he and Willie were related because of this and they spent most of the summer together.

Every Saturday afternoon, after school had finished, Robbie and Willie walked the four miles to Maybole. Willie's father was a shopkeeper there and Robbie loved spending the weekends in the rooms above the shop.

The Kirkoswald Fair was held every year in July. Robbie, who had already been taken to a few taverns by Willie, thought it would be a good idea to organise a dance at one of the taverns during the time of the Fair and invite girls along. Willie liked the idea too and arranged it with the tavern landlord.

The dance was a great success with a turnout of over twenty boys and girls – there was even a fiddler to play music. It was only as everyone started to leave that Robbie and Willie realised that no-one had any money to pay the landlord. Robbie did not even have a penny.

Luckily, Willie managed to persuade the landlord that he would pay the bill as soon as he could. The following Saturday, at home, Willie bought some pens and paper at a cheap price from his father. He and Robbie sold them at school the next week for a profit. It was enough to pay the tavern bill.

Robbie became used to seeing people drunk and fighting in the taverns and streets at night. Sometimes he went to the taverns with his friends. Although he never had much money to spend himself Robbie enjoyed watching everyone around him. It seemed a different life from the one he lived at Mount Oliphant. Robbie often thought of his father and how he would have disapproved of such behaviour.

It was his final week in Kirkoswald when he first saw Peggy Thomson who lived in the house next to the school. He had stepped out from his surveying lesson into the school garden to take a reading of the sun's altitude and there she was in her garden – a very pretty girl, just thirteen years old.

Robbie's heart began to beat faster and his pulse began to race. He had felt the same way on first seeing Nelly.

5. Lochlea Farm

ROBBIE, aged eighteen, was in love with a bonie lassie. She had the same name as his little sister – Isabella – but Robbie called her Tibbie.

His father, having reached agreements on his financial problems, had been able to leave Mount Oliphant and take over the running of Lochlea Farm. It was May when the family moved in.

The farm was almost three miles north-east of the village of Tarbolton and was set in bleak countryside surrounded by low hills. Although it had almost twice as much land as Mount Oliphant, the ground was marshy. William Burness decided to keep the old black cattle, raised for beef, at Lochlea rather than the Ayrshire breed which were well known for producing excellent milk. The Ayrshire breed needed good grazing which Lochlea, with its acres of swampy land, did not have.

Robbie walked to Tarbolton after work each day to meet Tibbie who lived in the village. Then the courtship ended almost as suddenly as it began.

Gilbert was always concerned because his brother seemed to fall in love so quickly and often and then seemed heartbroken when the courtships ended. Robbie had laughed about it one evening as he was writing a love letter to Tibbie and told Gilbert that he had a 'tinder heart' which was easily set alight.

Gilbert felt sorry for his brother as he had heard from the villagers that Robbie had knocked on Tibbie's door one evening, only to be told by her mother that her daughter was entertaining another gentleman.

'Poor Robbie, always the victim of some fair enslaver,' thought Gilbert.

Robbie's pride was hurt even more to find out later that Tibbie had come into money and obviously thought that she was now too fine a lady for the likes of him. Hurt and rejected, he threw himself into his reading after work each day.

On Sundays the whole family took the long walk to the village to attend the church services – one in the morning and one in the afternoon. Looking around during the church services, it was not long before Robbie started to cheer up again; there were plenty of other bonie lassies to fall in love with.

On market days Robbie, Gilbert, William and John all went with their father to the village to sell produce from the farm which mainly produced oats, barley and flax. The boys' mother, Agnes, always had a supply of fresh eggs, butter and small cheeses for them to sell.

Life at Lochlea was good. Robbie still had to work hard on the farm but he was used to it and just got on with the jobs, knowing that his father was getting older and could not work in the way he had before. At least, at Lochlea, Robbie could meet up with friends from neighbouring farms and the village. He soon became popular as he was a clever and amusing talker and often made up rhymes which his friends loved.

Robbie enjoyed the company of his friends so much that he decided to join the dancing class in the village. His father was not happy about this as he had noticed Robbie always had his eyes on the lassies and he preferred his son to stay at home. Robbie did not like displeasing his father, but he was twenty, not a boy any more, and he wanted to have fun. He liked dancing and thought the lessons would teach him how to behave correctly if ever he had the chance of invitations anywhere. Tibbie had obviously thought he was not good enough and Robbie was keen to better himself in any way he could. He also felt awkward and ungainly at times as his hard labour on the farm had given him round shoulders; secretly, he hoped that the dance lessons would improve his posture.

Robbie dressed in his own style, not cutting his hair short as his male friends did, but wearing his long dark hair tied back with a ribbon. Most of his friends wore grey-coloured plaids around their shoulders when they went out in the evening but his plaid was the colour of brown leaves in the autumn.

Robbie, enjoying life at Lochlea, became so confident, that by the time he reached the age of twenty one he planned to form his own club in Tarbolton. He decided it would be a gathering of his best friends which, at that time, meant Gilbert and five others.

Gilbert, who had once thought Robbie shy and bashful where the lassies were concerned, now thought him quite the 'lady's man' although he did not always agree with Robbie's idea of beauty. His older brother, once head-over-heels in love with some lassie or another, could never find any faults in them. Gilbert saw them as others did, without being blinded by the rosy glow of love. Gilbert, however, who was still quite shy, was excited when he heard his brother's plan.

'What will ye name it, Robert?'

'The Bachelors' Club*, of course. I have already worked out some rules for the club. It will be for young men, such as us, cheerful, honest-hearted lads.'

---

* At this time, meeting in public outside a church was regarded with suspicion by the authorities. Meeting to talk about the issues of the day was felt to be a threat to the government. These were the years of the Scottish Enlightenment and later the French Revolution when all received values and beliefs were brought into question. One

In the November of that year Robbie, true to his word, set up the club in an upstairs room of an alehouse in Tarbolton. The Bachelors' Club met once a month and held discussions for their entertainment. Robbie was elected president for the first meeting. That meeting and every one after was finished with a toast to the lassies they courted.

A few weeks after the first meeting of the Bachelors' Club Robbie fell in love with Elizabeth Gebbie. It did not surprise Gilbert to see that she was no real beauty but she did have a certain charm about her and she was quite clever.

Elizabeth was a daughter of a farmer who lived in the parish of Galston. Night after night saw Robbie arriving late back at Lochlea, the farm near Galston being a fair distance away. His late arrivals became frequent and late night stretched into the early hours of the morning. His heart was so full of love that he wrote rhymes about her to put his feelings into words. He called her Eliza.

Once, just as dawn was on the horizon, Robbie

Scottish radical Thomas Muir was tried for sedition for claiming that ordinary people should be allowed to vote and not just landowners. He was sentenced to deportation – forcibly removed – to Australia. Robert Burns's later poems show that justice and radical change were close to his own heart, especially when he wrote 'A Man's a Man'.

arrived back at Lochlea to find his father waiting up for him. William Burness was not pleased with his son's gallivanting and had stayed up to tell him plainly that such bad conduct would have to stop. He asked his son what had kept him out so late; Robbie made up such a story about the adventures he had encountered while on his way home that his father, enjoying the entertainment provided by his quick-witted son, forgot about his romancing. The romance continued.

Gilbert noticed that his brother was full of high spirits as he went about his work. One or two nights when Robbie could not visit Galston he practised playing on a violin he had bought for five shillings; his music-making did not sound good even though he could read music. His sister, Isabella, now a pretty girl of nine, would often sneak up to the attic when he was playing. There, in secret, by the light of a candle, she read in glee the poems she had taken out from the desk beside his bed.

A week or so later Robbie came home early in the evening, his face a picture of unhappiness. Gilbert took one look at his brother and guessed the cause immediately. The love of Robbie's life had broken his 'tinder heart'.

Davie Sillar, a friend of Gilbert who had joined the Bachelors' Club that year and often visited Lochlea, tried to console him when he heard that Eliza had

A MAN'S A MAN FOR A' THAT

Is there for honest Poverty
That hings his head, an' a' that;
The coward slave – we pass him by,
We dare be poor for a' that!
For a' that, an' a' that.
Our toils obscure an' a' that,
The rank is but the guinea's stamp,
The Man's the gowd for a' that.

What though on hamely fare we dine,
Wear hoddin grey, an' a that;
Gie fools their silks, and knaves their wine;
A man's a man for a' that:
For a' that, and a' that,
Their tinsel show, an' a' that;
The honest man, tho' e'er sae poor,
Is king o' men for a' that.

---

hing: hangs
gowd: gold
fare: food
hoddin: coarse woollen cloth
gie: give
tho': though
e'er: ever
sae: so

Ye see yon birkie, ca'd a lord,
Wha struts, an' stares, an' a' that;
Tho' hundreds worship at his word,
He's but a coof for a' that:
For a' that, an' a' that,
His ribband, star, an' a' that:
The man o' independent mind
He looks an' laughs at a' that.

A prince can mak a belted knight,
A marquis, duke, an' a' that;
But an honest man's abon his might,
Gude faith, he mauna fa' that!
For a' that, an' a' that,
Their dignities an' a' that;
The pith o' sense an' pride o' worth,
Are higher rank than a' that.

---

birkie: fellow
ca'd: called
coof: fool
o': of
abon: up above
maunna: mustn't

Then let us pray that come it may,
(As come it will for a' that,)
That Sense and Worth o'er a' the earth,
Shall bear the gree an' a' that.
For a' that, an' a' that,
It's coming yet for a' that,
That man to man, the world o'er,
Shall brithers be for a' that.

---

o'er: over
bear the gree: win the victory

rejected Robbie's love and proposal. He was a year younger than Robbie but he also knew how it felt to be rejected. Davie had fallen in love with a lassie called Margaret, who was working as a nursery maid at Stair House, one of the grand houses near Tarbolton.

When Davie visited his Meg, as he called her, he always took Robbie with him to act as chaperone because that was the local way of doing things. Meg liked Robbie and learned to sing some of the songs he had written when he left a few for her to look at.

Mrs. Stewart, the wealthy lady who owned Stair House, read the songs Meg showed her and enjoyed them too. She surprised everyone by inviting Robbie into the main drawing room to recite for her. Robbie felt very proud at not having to use the servants' entrance as he usually did. It was the first time he had ever entered a room with a Turkish carpet and although flattered, was embarrassed about his ragged shoes and appearance. Mrs. Stewart did not seem to glance twice at the way Robbie looked as he went over the songs for her and she praised him highly.

Davie looked up to Robbie and even tried to write rhymes as he did, although they could never match up to Robbie's. When he and Meg became engaged it was under the watchful eye of Robbie who had been chosen as a witness. The lovers exchanged a broken coin, held hands and swore to be true to one another. A short while later Meg broke off with Davie to court a shoemaker from Edinburgh.

Hearts full of misery the two rejected lovers went for a walk across the fields. Davie was thinking sadly of his Meg. Robbie, who always seemed to feel things more passionately than anyone else, was in agony at the loss of his lovely Eliza.

A RED RED ROSE

O, my luve's like a red, red rose,
    That's newly sprung in June.
O, my luve's like a melodie,
    That's sweetly play'd in tune.

As fair art thou, my bonie lass,
    So deep in luve am I,
And I will will luve thee still, my dear,
    Till a' the seas gang dry.

Till a' the seas gang dry, my dear,
    And the rocks melt wi' the sun!
O I will luve thee still, my dear,
    While the sands o' life shall run.

And fare thee weel, my only luve,
    And fare thee weel a while!
And I will come again, my luve,
    Tho' it were ten thousand mile!

6. Irvine

ROBBIE, now a young man of twenty two, was excited that summer as he made his way to Irvine, which was a big town some ten miles north of Lochlea. Gilbert had walked the first few miles with him to cheer him on his way but could only go so far as he had work to do. He headed back to the farm, turning a few times to watch Robbie until he could see him no more. Lochlea would not be the same without his elder brother.

Robbie had decided, after his last heartbreak, that he was going to take positive action towards planning his future. Two things were foremost in his mind.

One was that he wanted to seriously study a trade and the other was to better his position in society. Robbie had heard of an association which was much respected in the village as it did a lot of good for people in need. They called themselves Freemasons. Robbie wanted to be respected in the same way; he wanted to be a Freemason.

As far as the plan with learning a trade was concerned, he and Gilbert had already been growing flax on a piece of land they had rented from their father.

They had done quite well at selling it as the plants

were in demand. Thread and cloth such as linen, cambric, lawn and lace could be made from the stem fibres of the plant and linseed oil could be pressed from the seeds.

However, Robbie did not think that just growing flax was enough; he now wanted to learn more about the flax trade, especially the work carried out by a flax dresser which dealt with combing the plant's fibres straight before it was turned into linen.

Shortly before leaving Tarbolton, during the first week of July, Robbie attended a meeting in the little hall of the same alehouse where the Bachelors' Club was held. This was a Lodge meeting of the Freemasons – members of a secret order who had promised brotherly love and mutual assistance to one another.

Most of these men were tradesmen and profess-ional men of the district – skilled workmen, gentle-men, farmers and scholars. When Robbie arrived he noticed that a man had been placed at the door to guard the meeting while it was in progress. The fact that the meeting was held in such privacy excited Robbie and he wondered what was in store for him.

That evening, behind the guarded door, Robbie went through a special ritual to enter the order. He was dressed in special clothes and had to swear promises on the book, *The Volume of the Sacred Law*. As Robbie was a Christian, the book that was his *Volume of the Sacred Law* was the Holy Bible, which lay open on the table in the room.

Robbie placed his hand on it and swore that he believed in a Supreme Being and that he would always obey the law of his holy book and the law of his country. He promised to attend the Lodge whenever he was able and to be loyal to the other members. He promised to help any other person and their families in need of aid or charity if he was in a position to do so.

A few men at the meeting who knew Robbie said that he was a person of good character and they believed he would make a good freemason. It was with great pride that Robbie saw his name entered in the records as an apprentice.

As Robbie neared Irvine he thought of the night he became an apprentice in the Lodge. Feeling a heavy responsibility on his shoulders to be as good a citizen as possible and to help others whenever he could, he entered the town.

Robbie was surprised at the size and bustle of the streets in Irvine. The town was the main seaport handling goods for Glasgow. He had to cross the main street warily to avoid the many horses and carts jostling for room as they made their way to and from the harbour.

It took him a while to reach Glasgow Vennel, the place where he had arranged to lodge. There were so many interesting distractions in the town. Seagate

Castle, which had been visited by Mary, Queen of Scots, was one but what really excited him was the discovery of a good bookshop. A passer-by told him that it was the bookshop of William Templeton who was also a town councillor.

As he arrived at Glasgow Vennel and was walking down the cobbled street his nostrils were struck by a foul smelling odour that hung in the air. A woman who was approaching from the opposite direction started to wave at him. Robbie could see that she was nearing middle age and married as she wore a 'kertch' or headscarf, on her head.

'Rabbie Burns,' she called out, 'dinnae ye ken me laddie?'

It was then he recognised her. She was Mrs. Peacock who was married to his mother's half-brother, Alexander. Robbie had only seen them once or twice when he was very young. It was at their dwelling he was to stay and work as a flax dresser. As they reached the Peacocks' house and yard Robbie realised that the awful smell was coming from there.

Alexander Peacock was a rough, devious kind of man. Early that evening he spoke to Robbie for a while about the trade of flax-dressing, promising to teach Robbie all he knew about the business of manufacturing and retailing flax.

Robbie was keen to learn all he could. That night he slept on their kitchen floor. The next morning, full of enthusiasm, and trying to ignore the stink, he followed Alexander Peacock down to his yard outside to the heckling shop. This was where the flax-dressing was carried out.

As they left the brightness of the street and entered the shop it took Robbie a few moments to adjust his eyes to the gloom and the cloud of dust that was floating all around the place. For an instant he thought of his open fields with the blue sky above him as he worked on the farm and wondered how he would feel working in this small, rancid, noisy, stuffy room in such dim light. He noticed a man who was laying some fibres over a board and furiously beating the seeds off them with a long knife-like tool. Alexander Peacock followed Robbie's gaze.

'Yon's scutching,' he shouted 'wi a scutching knife.' Robbie nodded.

'Yon man's heckling,' he added pointing to another man in the corner, 'wi a heckle.'

Robbie watched as the man used two different kinds of boards with long, sharp iron prongs on each to straighten the fibres and separate the short strands from the long ones. It all seemed a different world to the one he was used to. Robbie suppressed a sigh as Alexander Peacock showed him where he was to sleep from then on – in the adjoining room which was used as a stable and a storage place. The bed was in the loft.

A few weeks later Robbie could feel that his spirits were low. He began dreading the opening of the shop door every morning as he reached it. The smell hanging over the yard as he approached made him feel sick. Learning the flax trade was not at all the exciting adventure he had imagined. His headaches were becoming frequent again and he missed the fresh air he had been used to.

As soon as he could Robbie found new lodgings further down the Vennel. He rented an attic room in a tenement for one shilling a week. It did not take him long to suspect that Alexander Peacock was a rogue and he decided to keep a close eye on him.

In August the town celebrated its annual festival of Marymass. The Saturday of the festival brought warm, sunny weather with it as well as even more bustle for the town than was usual. Stalls and carts, brightly coloured and decorated with banners, had been set up early that morning with their wares on display ready for the expected crowd of local people. Many others who lived within travelling distance of the town would be sure to arrive before the afternoon. Splendidly adorned horses and their riders made their way through the gathering crowd of men, women and over-excited children to prepare for the procession towards the moor where the races were to be held.

Vendors cried out at the tops of their voices to attract customers, their shouts competing with the stirring sound of a lively band of marching trumpeters and drummers. Robbie was not in a mood for any of the festivity. The work at the heckling shop had been getting him down and he felt so depressed that even the sunny day and the excitement all around him could not cheer him up. His head was beginning to pound again as he screwed his eyes up in the sunshine, the noise in the street was becoming unbearable, his joints ached and he could not get the thought of Eliza out of his mind.

He returned to his attic room but even there the noise carried on until dawn, signalling the end of the Marymass and the arrival of the Sabbath day.

Robbie tried to console himself whenever he had the time by visiting his new friend, John Hamilton, who was a son of the Provost at Irvine. Sometimes he called into William Templeton's bookshop where he could forget all his troubles for a while reading new ballads at the counter in the shop or memorising poems of Robert Fergusson, a young Scottish man who had tragically died in Edinburgh some seven years before. Robbie had not written any poems for a while but these poems, which were new to him, gave him inspiration to try his writing again. He wrote with renewed fervour, but many of his poems contained feelings of sadness within them.

October came and Robbie's low spirits became even worse. He slept badly at night, often waking suddenly, bathed in sweat and with his heart beating wildly. He remembered that his mother had placed his feet in a bowl of cool water when the same kind of fever had broken his sleep as a boy. He tried that again and although it calmed him a little for a short time, the broken nights of sleep continued. It was an effort for him to get up each day and even more of an effort to make his way to the heckling shop which he had grown to hate. The following month he took to his bed with a raging fever.

William Burness, busy with his farming at Lochlea despite a persistent cough which he could not seem to be rid of, forgot his own problems when he heard from a visitor that Robbie was very ill. Leaving everything in the capable hands of Gilbert, and ignoring the coldness of the weather, he saddled his best horse and made his way to Irvine.

When he arrived in the town, he left his horse in the care of a local farrier and hurried to the tenement where Robbie was lodged. He arrived there just as another man was climbing the wooden staircase which led to Robbie's attic room. The man introduced himself as Surgeon Fleming, the local doctor, who had already visited his patient a number of times. At first the doctor had prescribed *ipecacuanha* and then a *sacred elixir* to clear out his patient's insides, then a painkiller to ease the inflammation of the joints. Finally, as was usual in treating high fevers, he used powdered *cinchona*.

Robbie was lying in bed looking pale and exhausted. His father was relieved to see that the fever had passed although it was clear that his son was in a lot of pain as he struggled to sit up.

'Robin, Robin!' was all he could utter.

Robbie noticed, with gratitude, the concern and sympathy in his father's face. To him, that felt better than any tonic the doctor could give.

Robbie returned to the heckling shop as soon as he was able. He had already decided not to visit his family for Christmas or Hogmanay as he wanted to catch up with lost time at his work. On the 27th of December he wrote a letter to his father explaining that he was still feeling depressed but was taking each day as it came and not dwelling on the past or thinking too seriously of the future.

Alexander Peacock and his wife were in a mood to celebrate at Hogmanay. They had already taken a few drinks in the heckling shop and invited Robbie to join them in their celebrations. Robbie tried to ignore the unpleasant surroundings and after one or two glasses of port relaxed a bit. He was just beginning to enjoy himself for the first time in ages when Mrs. Peacock, who had drunk far too much earlier in the day, lost her balance when reaching for a bottle and knocked over a candle as she did so.

The shop full of dust caught fire at once. There was not a thing anyone could do. Alexander Peacock, with Robbie's help, pushed and pulled Mrs. Peacock outside. They watched in disbelief from the safe distance of the malt shop across the street as it burned to ashes.

Robbie walked to his lodging in the early hours of the New Year's morning wondering what on earth he was going to do now. By the time his twenty third birthday arrived on the 25th of that month Robbie was feeling more optimistic. He had hated the heckling shop and not liked Alexander Peacock at all, finding him a cheat and a scoundrel.

'O why the deuce should I repine, and be an ill-forboder? I'm twenty-three, and five-feet-nine, – I'll go and be a sodger!' he sang to himself and feeling much better went out to see what he could do to improve things. The day seemed even better when he read a copy of *The Glasgow Mercury* newspaper at the bookshop. The front page listed farmers who had won a prize from the government for flax growing. Near the bottom of the list he read that Robert Burns, farmer, Lochlea Farm, Tarbolton, Ayrshire, had been awarded a premium of £3 for growing 3 acres of flax.

In great spirits he made contact with another heckling shop in Montgomery Boyd's Close with the intention of completing his training and paid seven shillings to cover the next three months.

Shortly after he met a man called Richard Brown. Robbie had just left a freemasons' meeting at the Harbour Lodge with some of the other members.

Standing outside was his friend, a clerk at a local lawyer's office. Robbie and others nicknamed this clerk Keelivine, the name meaning a lead pencil.

They decided to escape the cold January weather by heading to the nearby Wheat Sheaf Inn to warm up with a hot toddy. As they were sitting near the open fire enjoying their whisky toddies Richard Brown joined them. Robbie had noticed him around the town once or twice before. He spoke first to Keelivine, who already knew him, and then introduced himself to Robbie.

After that the group often met at the Wheat Sheaf. Robbie was fascinated by Richard who was some six years older. He told amazing tales of his adventures as a sailor. Not long before they met he had been set ashore in Ireland by an American Privateer who had stripped him of everything he owned. Privateers seemed to be almost the same as pirates to Robbie. These stories brought back memories of the smugglers he had heard of on the shore at Kirkoswald.

He had thought that exciting at the time but Robbie could not hear enough of Richard's experiences at sea and in other countries. He was all attention to learn. He stopped going to the heckling shop each day to spend hours strolling around the town with his new friend.

Richard, being older and more travelled, taught Robbie of places and things he had never heard of and boasted of the many ladies he had romanced during his adventures. There had been some who had loved him and some who had broken his heart. Many of the ladies he spoke of, especially the ones who hung about the sailors in ports or taverns, did not sound very ladylike to Robbie.

He did not understand how Richard could be so flippant about heartbreak but his friend just laughed saying that he was a fool as far as women were concerned. Robbie wished he could take heartbreak so easily – he still felt the pain of his rejection by Eliza.

As the weather improved they lengthened their walks. One Sunday the two decided to go to Eglinton Woods. The woods were scattered with carpets of snowdrops and a light fall of snow on that day but they were more intent on their conversation than on the scenery around them. Robbie, desperately wanting to impress his friend, recited verses of his poetry in the hope that Richard would like them.

Richard listened carefully and said he was surprised that Robbie had not sent such good verses to a magazine. The idea had never occurred to Robbie before. That night as he sat in his room and went over the things they had talked about he thought of what Richard had said about the verses. It made him think of a new ambition. Robbie wondered if he could ever become a poet.

7. Mossgiel

ROBBIE and Gilbert decided to look for another farm. It was obvious that their father, who had suffered a terrible illness for some months, would not live much longer. The brothers, knowing that the family's future would soon be in their hands, wanted to be sure they had a new home to move into.

William Burness died in February 1784; in March the family moved to Mossgiel which was some three miles from Lochlea in the neighbouring parish of Mauchline. Gavin Hamilton, who was a lawyer and a freemason in the parish, rented his farm to them for £90 a year. He had leased it from the Earl of Loudon, wanting to use the farm as a summer retreat, but his wife had not liked the idea.

When Robbie asked to lease it from him he readily agreed. Hamilton was always keen to help another freemason if he could. The farm had 118 acres of land and had been well stocked. Robbie and Gilbert were each to receive a yearly wage of £7.

The farmhouse was no bigger than their old one having a 'but' and 'ben' and an attic. The attic had three small rooms. Robbie and Gilbert shared the middle one.

The land at Mossgiel seemed a little better than at

Lochlea as it was not so full of stones but the earth was still marshy. Drainage was just as much a problem in their new venture as it had been on their old farm.

Matters had not gone well at the start; the frosty weather had been against them, the first Spring there had arrived late and the seed Robbie had bought for sowing was of poor quality. He had set out with good intentions. He read farming books, calculated crops and visited as many markets as he could in order to learn as much as possible. His spirits were high and he was full of optimism for the future.

Encouraged by Gilbert he also returned to his writing that year with enthusiasm. Each day as Robbie worked in the fields he thought of the places and people he knew and of the goings on in town, of the quarrels of neighbours, the preaching of ministers at church, the bonie lassies and their romancing. As he guided the plough he thought of his family and the troubles they had endured.

Sometimes he stopped for a moment just to look around and take in the scenery and happenings around him; a hare racing across the field, a murder of crows darkening the sky above, a tiny flower growing in a waste of muddy rills. Through the long days he often thought of his father, a humble farmer, whose life had always been a struggle in his efforts to give his children a good education and a better chance for their future.

As soon as he was able, after the day's work Robbie sat at a desk in his attic room and wrote down these thoughts. Some of them were already verses in his mind, others he wrote and rewrote until he was happy with the result.

One day some months later as the brothers were working hard in the kail yard and had taken a break for a moment, Robbie recited his latest verses to Gilbert to see what he thought of them.

'In my opinion, Robbie,' he said, 'those verses would bear being printed.'

It was an exciting idea and that night as they lay in their beds in the darkness of the attic room, the brothers talked of sending the verses to a magazine.

Finally they stopped talking and Gilbert fell asleep. But Robbie's mind was too fired up to let him sleep. He kept thinking of what Richard Brown had said when they had walked in Eglinton Woods near Irvine. As he eventually started drifting off to sleep Robbie resolved to work hard on his poetry.

He had been reading a great deal at Mossgiel but now decided to read even more. He liked the works of the Scottish poets best; his favourite being Robert Fergusson. He remembered, with fondness, the times he had spent browsing through books and ballads in William Templeton's bookshop where he had first found the works of the Edinburgh poet. He wondered if his verses could ever be as good.

The people of Mauchline were beginning to know him as a rhymer but Robbie dreamt of being known as more than that. Sighing heavily, he turned over in bed. There was a heavy day's work ahead; the magazines and his fame would have to wait.

That summer, Gilbert, finally overcoming his shyness, had started to court a girl called Jean who lived on a nearby farm while Robbie romanced a servant girl called Betsy who had worked for his mother at Lochlea the winter past. His affair with Betsy did not last long as he realised that he was not in love with her.

For once, Gilbert was the one to feel the hurt of rejection when Jean broke up with him to court another farmer. Harvest time arrived proving Robbie right in his concern over the seed he had purchased for sowing; the harvest was a bad one. On top of this, in October, Robbie received news that the farm girl he had been meeting with that summer was now expecting his child.

His mother was angry with him and said he should marry the poor girl. Gilbert and Robbie's sisters, Agnes and Annabella, were horrified at the thought of Betsy Paton becoming Robbie's wife. They considered her plain, unladylike and not at all what they had in mind for their brother. Robbie boasted to John Rankine, a neighbouring farmer, that he would soon be a father but secretly was embarrassed at the situation he now found himself in.

He was not in love with Betsy and had never promised to wed. In the end he decided not to marry her but to help with the child if needed. He and Gilbert threw themselves back into the farm work to try to make up for the poor harvest and the bad luck that seemed to lie over them at Mossgiel.

The biting winds and hard ground of November arrived. Robbie had spent an exhausting day with Gilbert and William, trying to drain a section of land. William was seventeen. He had been keen to show his older brothers that he could work as well as any man. Robbie was proud of his efforts and told him so. It reminded him of the days he had first taken the plough for his father even though he had been just twelve at the time. He was always patient and cheerful with all the young folk working on the farm, even if they made mistakes or worked too slowly. Gilbert was the one who told them off.

That night, as Robbie sat at his desk writing by the flickering light of a candle, he was thinking of his father as he wrote:

November chill blaws loud wi' angry sugh
The short'ning winter-day is near a close
The miry beasts retreating frae the pleugh
The black'ning trains o' craws to their repose
The toil-worn Cotter frae his labor goes
This night his weekly moil is at an end
Collects his spades, his mattocks, and his hoes
Hoping the morn in ease and rest to spend
And weary, o'er the moor, his course does
                                hameward bend.

The following year brought cold frosty weather again. In January Robbie's friend, John Richmond, had to stand up in church to be shamed in front of the congregation as the minister lectured him for getting his girlfriend Jenny pregnant. Robbie tried to persuade John to marry her, even though he had decided against marrying Betsy Paton. John was in no mood to take his older friend's advice; he had set his mind on going to Edinburgh.

Spring arrived late as it had the previous year, with Robbie and his brothers and sisters resuming the usual cycle of long hard days and hours of toil on the farm.

When April arrived a Penny dance was held at the end of Race Week at Mauchline. It was called a Penny dance because the fiddler was paid a penny for each reel he played. Robbie remembered how his father had forbidden him to go to dancing lessons when they lived at Lochlea Farm; now his poor father was dead. He felt sorry that he had disobeyed him; however Robbie had to admit that he still loved dancing and was good at it. A dance in the town was too good an opportunity to miss.

THE BELLES OF MAUCHLINE*

In Mauchline there dwells six proper young belles,
The pride of the place and its neighbourhood a';
Their carriage and dress, a stranger would guess,
In Lon'on or Paris, they'd gotten it a'.

Miss Miller is fine, Miss Markland's divine,
Miss Smith she has wit, and Miss Betty is braw:
There's beauty and fortune to get wi' Miss Morton;
But Armour's the jewel for me o' them a'.

---

* Robert Burns knew the six young ladies from
Mauchline. They were Helen (Nell) Miller, Jean
Markland, Jean Smith, Elizabeth (Bess, Betty)
Miller, Christina Morton and Jean Armour.
Robbie courted several of these ladies.
braw: fine, well-dressed

By this time Robbie was getting to know a girl called Bess Miller, a kind and pleasant girl who sympathised with the many problems he had met with at Mossgiel. He and Gilbert met her, along with her sister Nell, and together they made their way to the dance which was held in a hall in the town near the old Castle.

The hall, which was really not much more than a barn, was packed with young men and women. Robbie knew some of them and greeted them warmly as he entered the hall. Bess and Nell also met some of their friends and Robbie noted, with the eye he always had for a pretty lassie, that a few were quite bonie.

Everyone thought it funny when Robbie's young dog, who had followed him to the dance, started weaving skilfully between the legs of the dancers to keep as close to its master as possible. Robbie was very fond of his new young collie. His last dog, Luath, had disappeared the night before Robbie's father had died. It had wandered off Lochlea Farm and a neighbouring farmer cruelly killed it.

Robbie laughed at the little dog tailing his dance steps and said it was 'a gash and faithfu' tyke'. He had said the same of Luath. He commanded the dog to go home and playfully remarked that he wished he could find a lass who would love him as faithfully as his little dog did.

A few days later, the weather being bright and fine,

Robbie made his way to Gavin Hamilton's house. He wanted to discuss some business to do with Betsy Paton. As he was crossing the village green he passed several young girls who were spreading washing out on the grass to dry in the fresh air. The same little dog that followed him everywhere ran on the clean clothes. One of the girls scolded the dog and threw a small stone at it.

Robbie stopped in his tracks and stared hard at her.

'Lassie,' he said sternly, 'if ye thought ought o' me, ye wadna hurt my dog!'

He walked on calling the dog to his heel. He remembered seeing the girl in the town several times before. The last time had been at the dance; she was a friend of Bess Miller.

He turned his head to take another look at the girl. She was not overly pretty but tall and shapely, with long dark brown hair tied back in a pony tail. She was still watching him and muttering something to herself. Robbie could not help smiling as she hastily turned her head and pretended to be busy with the washing.

'A bonie lassie,' he confided to his dog, 'a bonie sonsie lassie.'

Towards the end of May, news arrived at Mossgiel to say that Betsy Paton had given birth to a baby girl; she had been named Elizabeth.

The following month Bess Miller, who was looking forward to her brother's wedding in July, was embarrassed when she heard about Betsy Paton's baby. She and her sisters had been very excited about the wedding because William was marrying a wealthy heiress called Agnes Bell. Now instead of telling people she met about the beautiful clothes she was going to wear at the wedding she had to avoid their eyes because she knew they were thinking about Robbie and Betsy Paton.

Although she had not been courting Robbie for long, she decided to break off with him.

His 'tinder heart' was upset yet again but Robbie could understand why Bess left him and, if the truth really be told, he was beginning to think more and more about the lassie he had met on the washing green.

He had asked some of his friends about her and knew that her name was Jean and that she was the eldest daughter of a master stonemason who lived in Mauchline. His friend, James Smith, told him that Jean's father was very strict and kept a close eye on anyone who might be interested in his daughter. Robbie had just laughed and told James 'for a' that, love would e'er find a way'.

For a second year the harvest had been late in coming and half the crop had failed. Robbie tried to push the frustration of the poor harvest to the back of his mind as he gave wee Bess a kiss and handed her to his mother who was waiting to put her to bed. The baby had been at the farm for a full month, ever since she had been weaned.

Betsy Paton had found work on another farm so it suited her fine to hand the baby over to be raised by the family at Mossgiel. The whole family sat in the house that evening discussing the events that had led to such a poor harvest. It had not been the seed this time; they all agreed it had been the weather, the lingering frost and late summer. They were very disappointed as they had all worked so hard.

Robbie could hardly look them in the eye. He could see that Gilbert was thinking very hard. He knew that his brother, always so sensible and level-headed about matters, was already working out the most practical way of balancing their losses. William and John, fine young men, were promising their mother that they would double their efforts to help in the coming seasons while his three sisters added their cries of comfort and support.

He was the eldest and should take the lead in providing for the family but Robbie felt he had failed them. He knew that Gilbert would never give up on farming but he had lost his faith in it.

The long days of back-breaking work at the plough, hours of draining land, of clearing rocks, weeding, spreading manure, herding cattle, constantly fighting the inclement weather – what had they amounted to? Nothing!

The more Robbie thought about his future in farming, the more the enthusiasm he had felt on first moving to Mossgiel lessened. He doubted that he would ever be successful as a farmer. Feeling as if he had a heavy weight on his shoulders Robbie climbed the steps to his room in the attic and sat down at his desk to think in the dark.

In the room below he heard the sound of wee Bess crying, and then he heard his sister, Isabella, singing softly. His mother's voice joined hers. For just a moment the lullaby took him back in his mind to Alloway, to the 'auld clay biggin' his father had built. The baby's crying stopped as he stood up.

'Thou's welcome wean!' he whispered to his little baby in the room below, 'I'll be a loving father to thee and brag o't.'

He sat back down again, put a lit taper to the candle on his desk and started to write a poem for his new daughter. He was pleased with it when it was finished and leaned back in his chair with a smile on his face.

Then his thoughts wandered to Jean. He had been courting her for a number of weeks now. Her father did not know a thing about it. Robbie's smile grew wider as he remembered how he had first flirted with Jean by calling to her from an open window at the back of the Whitefoord Arms. The tavern stood in a narrow lane opposite James Armour's house. Robbie had started a club at the tavern with his friends, John Richmond, James Smith and William Hunter. They

WHISTLE AN' I'LL COME TO YE, MY LAD*

O whistle, an' I'll come to ye, my lad,
O whistle, an' I'll come to ye, my lad:
Tho' father an' mother an' a' should gae mad,
O whistle, an' I'll come to ye, my lad.

But warily tent, when ye come to court me,
And come nae unless the back-yett be a-jee;
Syne up the back style and let naebody see,
And come as ye were na comin' to me.
And come as ye were na comin' to me.

At kirk, or at market, whene'er ye meet me,
Gang by me as tho' that ye car'd na a flie;
But steal me a blink o' your bonie black e'e,
Yet look as ye were na lookin' to me.
Yet look as ye were na lookin' to me.

---

* Written about Robert Burns and Jean Armour
secretly courting in the face of her family's wishes.
Tho': though
a': all
tent: take care
na: not:
yett: gate,
a-jee: ajar
syne: then
stile: steal, creep
kirk: church
gang: go
car'd: cared
e'e: eye

Ay vow and protest that ye care na for me,
And whiles ye may lightly my beauty a wee;
But court na anither, tho' jokin' ye be,
For fear that she wyle your fancy frae me.
For fear that she wyle your fancy frae me.

O whistle, an' I'll come to ye, my lad,
O whistle, an' I'll come to ye, my lad:
Tho' father an' mother an' a' should gae mad,
O whistle, an' I'll come to ye, my lad.

Ay: always
a wee: a little
wyle: entice
frae: from

jokingly named it The Court of Equity with Robbie being the chairman.

He had met Jean in secret often since then. Jean had a young brother, Adam, who was just fourteen. He thought their secret love affair was very exciting and enjoyed the task of delivering love letters from Robbie at Mossgiel to his sister, especially when Robbie paid him for doing it. In return Jean wrote messages to Robbie to say where they could next meet without being seen. Robbie's smile faded away as he thought of James Armour. He knew Jean's father did not like him one bit and hoped the stonemason would not discover their romance.

Just as he snuffed the candle to go to bed Gilbert came into the room. The two undressed by the light of the moon which was shining through the window in the roof. They spoke for a while about different things, mostly about baby Bess. Neither of them mentioned the poor harvest.

In October John felt unwell and had to take to his bed. Robbie watched in horror as his youngest brother became really sick and the doctor was called for. Wee Bess's three aunts kept her well away from her sick uncle as a precaution.

Robbie's mother spent every minute of each day and night nursing her youngest son and everyone prayed that he would soon get better. But two days from the month's end, as Robbie was trying to repair a broken shaft on a cart with Gilbert and William, the unthinkable happened. They saw Isabella running towards them for all she was worth. She was crying her heart out. John had died.

November brought his funeral, not the best that money could buy but the best that they could manage. All that month Robbie felt as though his mind was in a daze.

He had carried on his work as usual but it seemed to him that his body was working independently of his mind. He started tasks and finished those without even realising that time had passed. The fog filled his head until, one day, as he was ploughing, he turned up the nest of a tiny field mouse.

His gaudsman, John, whose job it was to urge on the team of horses, went after the mouse to kill it, but Robbie angrily shouted after him to let it be. As he returned to his plough, Robbie considered the mouse and the work it must have done to build its nest as a shelter against the cold weather; all to no purpose.

The fog clouding his thoughts began to clear. Suddenly he felt as if he understood the sadness that depressed him, losing his father, losing his brother of course, but it was more than that; much more. It was the constant struggle for existence, the trying hard to achieve and still not succeeding, the many failures behind and the not knowing what was to come.

That night, at his desk in the attic room, he put his feelings into words. The wee mouse had suffered a terrible calamity that day but Robbie felt his life was one long run of misfortune.

TO A MOUSE, ON TURNING HER UP IN HER NEST WITH THE PLOUGH, NOVEMBER, 1785

Wee sleekit, cow'rin', tim'rous beastie,
O, what a panic's in thy breastie!
Thou need na start awa sae hasty,
Wi' bickering brattle!
I wad be laith to rin an' chase thee,
Wi' murdering pattle!

I'm truly sorry man's dominion
Has broken Nature's social union,
An' justifies that ill opinion,
Which makes thee startle
At me, thy poor earth-born companion,
An' fellow mortal!

I doubt na, whyles, but thou may thieve;
What then? poor beastie, thou maun live!
A daimen icker in a thrave
'S a sma' request:

---

sleekit: smooth
brattle: scurry
laith: loth, unwilling
pattle: a plough spade
whyles: sometimes
maun: must
a daimen icker: an odd ear of corn
thrave: 24 sheaves of corn

I'll get a blessin' wi' the lave,
An' never miss't!

Thy wee bit housie, too, in ruin;
Its silly wa's the win's are strewin'!
An' naething, now, to big a new ane,
O' foggage green!
An' bleak December's win's ensuin',
Baith snell and keen!

Thou saw the fields laid bare an' waste,
An' weary winter comin' fast,
An' cozie here, beneath the blast,
Thou thought to dwell,
'Till, crash! the cruel coulter past
Out thro' thy cell.

---

lave: the rest, the remainder
wa's: walls
win's: winds
foggage green: rough grass
baith: both
snell: chilly
coulter: the blade of a plough

That wee bit heap o' leaves an' stibble,
Has cost thee mony a weary nibble!
Now thou's turned out, for a' thy trouble,
But house or hald,
To thole the winter's sleety dribble,
An' cranreuch cauld!

But mousie thou art no thy lane
In proving foresight may be vain:
The best laid schemes o' mice an' men,
Gang aft agley,
An' lea'e us nought but grief an' pain,
For promis'd joy.

Still thou art blest, compar'd wi' me!
The present only toucheth thee:
But, och! I backward cast my e'e,
On prospects drear!
An' forward, tho' I canna see,
I guess an' fear.

---

stibble: stubble
but: without
hald: shelter
thole: suffer, endure
cranreuch: hoarfrost
thy lane: alone
gang agley: go wrong
aft: often
lea'e: leave
e'e: eye

8. Cruel Fate

THERE was talk in the town. Robbie had noticed more heads than usual turning to watch him as he walked down the street, or huddling in small groups to whisper outside the kirk.

He had told Gilbert, of course, and his friend William Hunter one night in the Whitefoord Arms as he knew he could trust them. John Richmond was still in Edinburgh staying away from Jenny. James Smith also left Mauchline just before Christmas after discovering his mother's servant was expecting his baby.

Jean had met Robbie secretly the night before in a panic as she was sure her parents would soon notice if other people already had. He tried to calm her as best he could and even wrote a letter to say that he, Robert Burns, would always love and support his Jean Armour. The letter seemed to soothe her and she was still hugging it tightly as she made her way home.

Robbie sighed deeply. He knew that Jean's parents would soon find out that she was expecting a baby. Jean had first told him two months after Christmas. Robbie's feelings had been muddled. He had been excited as he really loved Jean but he knew that there would be problems with her father. He even began to think that it would be better if he left the town, went to another country even – like Jamaica. Many men went to Jamaica and some made their fortunes there. Perhaps he could make a fortune and be able to look after Jean and the baby. Then he thought of how his friend John Richmond had left Jenny and how broken poor Jenny had been. He could not do that to his bonie Jean.

All the same, it would not do any harm, Robbie decided, to try to bring in some extra money. If he married Jean it would help them. He hoped he would be able to marry her but was very worried about her father's response. James Armour was so set in his ways and really strict about his children's behaviour. He did not like Robbie at all, thinking him too poor a farmer to marry his favourite daughter. The stone-mason was a proud and stubborn man who liked his old fashioned values and the old ways of running the kirk. He despised Robbie's modern ways of thinking and the fact that he was not afraid to speak his mind.

Robbie told Gilbert what was in his mind and his brother agreed that there would be trouble from James Armour.

'Foiragainst ye wed, Robin, ye had best be set for running afore he sets the law on ye. Yon will hae ye in the jile as soon as spare ye a glance.'

Robbie frowned as Gilbert voiced the words he

had been thinking himself. He really wanted to marry his Jean but if her father acted against it he would have no choice. If the law decided he was in the wrong there was, indeed, the risk that he could be sent to jail. He would have to hide until he could leave the country.

That night, in their room in the attic, the two brothers sat huddled over the small desk and worked out a plan of action if James Armour would not give his permission for Robbie to marry Jean.

'Ye will hae need o' money,' Gilbert whispered and he opened the lid of the desk.

They both stared for a moment at all the poems Robbie had written. As Robbie began to lift them out Gilbert found string to tie them into a bundle.

Early the next morning Robbie visited Gavin Hamilton and told him of the plan to escape to the West Indies if the need arose. The lawyer thought publishing his poems as soon as possible would be a good way of raising money for the ship's passage and advised him to tell his friends so that they would all buy a copy.

During the last week of March Gavin Hamilton took Robbie to a meeting of the Masonic lodge in Loudon parish to introduce him to the freemasons there. Robbie already knew one or two of them but the others were new acquaintances. He told them all that he intended to take his poems to the printer at

Kilmarnock. Some of them knew the printer whose name was John Wilson. By the time April arrived he was feeling hopeful that he would get his poems published and sell enough copies to make some money. He could hardly wait to tell Jean.

Robbie went to the house of James Armour to ask how Jean was and hopefully to see her. Her mother answered the door. On seeing who it was she spat out what she thought of him and slammed the door in his face.

Robbie felt humiliated at what Jean's mother had called him and for a moment was taken back to the time when Eliza's mother had slammed the door in his face. By the time he had reached Mossgiel he was angrier than he had ever been in his life before.

He was angry at Jean's parents for not thinking him good enough to marry their daughter. He was angry at the cruel way fate had made him a poor farmer. He was angry at the way that things turned out bad no matter how hard he tried. He was angry with the world and he was angry with life.

Jean's mother had returned to her sitting room shaking with indignation. The audacity of that upstart coming to her door!

She remembered with horror the night Jean had told her father she was expecting a baby. Her husband had fainted, only coming to after she had dosed him with some cordial. Then Jean told him the father was Robert Burns and he had exploded with rage.

'Robert Mossgiel, Robert Mossgiel!' he raged, 'Dinnae tell me it is Robert Mossgiel – ye ken how I hate the man.'

Jean mumbled words to the effect that he was not that bad. She had sheepishly shown her father the letter Robbie had written which promised that 'he, Robert Burns would always love and support his Jean Armour'. This did nothing to help. Her father held the letter at arm's length as if it had been poison and groaned out loud as he read the words Robbie had painstakingly written down.

Mary Armour, still feeling unsteady on her legs as she thought of that dreadful night, sat down and started to cry. If only that upstart had known Jean was no longer in the house.

It was just a matter of days before Robbie found out. Adam Armour turned up at Mossgiel wide-eyed and out of breath. He had been involved in a silly prank with some of his teenage friends and begged Robbie to let him lay low at his farm until the scandal died down.

Robbie, always sympathetic towards the young, took Adam in. He asked how his sister was keeping and it was then Adam told him that Jean had been sent away by her father.

'She's wi' Uncle Andrew and Aunt Lizzie in Paisley,' he added.

Robbie felt sorry for Jean, but he knew that the whole town must be talking about them and it would be better for her not to be a part of that. He was really missing her but glad that she was out of the reach of gossiping Mauchline tongues. He was more determined than ever to make some money so that he could care for Jean and the baby.

Robbie set off for Kilmarnock with his poems wrapped in a parcel under his arm. The town lay some nine miles from Mauchline. He found the printing works in the attics of the tenement on the left hand side of the Star Inn Close.

John Wilson liked the poems well enough but was wary about risking his good money on publishing them. He advised Robbie to ask as many people as he could to promise to buy copies if they were published. Over the next few weeks Robbie visited or wrote to his friends asking them to subscribe to the poetry publication. Matters seemed to be going well for a change and Robbie was pleased with the way the number of subscriptions was growing. On the 14th of April he was delighted to receive the proposal sheets from John Wilson.

However the next day found Robbie in a foul mood. He heard that James Armour had taken the letter of his promise to Jean to a solicitor in Ayr. Robbie knew this solicitor; he was Robert Aiken, a man who liked his poetry and had helped him to gain many subscribers for the poems.

Jean's father had demanded that the names on the letter be cut out. James Armour wanted Robert Burns out of his daughter's life for good and saw this as a legal way of doing it.

Robbie thought it incredible that Jean's father could hate him so much and was missing Jean more than ever. As if things were not bad enough he could not believe his ears when he heard that his bonie Jean had borrowed money from a young man who had visited her at her uncle's house several times.

Furious, he questioned Adam who nervously admitted that the man was a Mauchline man, Robert Wilson, working as a weaver in Paisley.

The hatred of James Armour was one thing; but to be betrayed by his beloved Jean was too much for him to bear.

Robbie stormed out of the house with such a black look on his face that Adam fearfully called Gilbert to tell him what had just happened. Gilbert went running after his brother in concern; but Robbie was nowhere to be seen.

As he stood looking into the distance hoping against hope to catch a glimpse of Robbie, Gilbert felt an awful chill of dread running down his back. He had seen his brother's 'tinder heart' broken before but this time – this time he knew that it had been shattered into pieces.

Robbie arrived home the next evening. Gilbert was

still working, tending to the horses, when his brother, looking worse than he had ever seen him before, strode up to his favourite stallion. Robbie picked up a curry comb and casually started to brush the horse's flanks to loosen the mud that had caked its hair. He stopped once or twice to hit the comb on the back of his boots to clear the dirt. Gilbert chatted lightly about how the horses had worked well that day. When they had stabled the horses for the night the two brothers went into the farmhouse. Their mother took one look at Robbie and busied herself with filling a bowl of broth for him to eat. Even Isabella could see that Robbie's spirits were low and it was only after she had placed wee Bess on his lap that he seemed to relax a bit. No-one mentioned Jean.

William told Gilbert that he would take over Robbie's work to give him time to get over his heartbreak but Gilbert thought that was a bad idea. Work would keep Robbie busy and perhaps keep his mind off things.

So it was, the days carried on as usual, only Robbie no longer sang as he worked or quipped with the young helpers. The nights were not the same. Soon after work each evening Robbie left the farm and did not return until the early hours of each morning. His mother watched him anxiously as he wandered off towards the town. She knew he was drinking more than was good for him and prayed that Robbie would soon come to his senses.

The month of May saw Robbie away from the farm for days at a time. Gilbert suspected that his brother had found a new girl but Robbie did not talk to him about his life in the way he used to.

In June Robbie had to sit in the kirk for three Sundays in a row while the ministers scolded him over his affair with Jean Armour. This punishment in public over, Robbie turned his mind again to Jamaica. He decided to hand his share of Mossgiel over to Gilbert to prevent James Armour claiming any of his property.

'This way the bairn is safe,' he said to Gilbert who had promised to raise wee Bess while Robbie was away.

The two looked at one another as if they could hardly believe what was happening to their lives. Over the next week Robbie had to leave Mossgiel several times to hide at friends' houses. James Armour had taken out a warrant for his arrest. As he had predicted, he was threatened with jail.

Robbie could see no future for himself in Scotland and was sure that his only way out of all his troubles was to emigrate.

Then on the last day of July he heard that his poems had been published in Kilmarnock. Slowly, from the innermost part of his mind, an old thought began to form again.

The thought grew clearer until his mind became

full of it. He recognised it as the dream of his younger
days; the dream of being known as more than a
rhymer. The dream of being a great bard of Scotland
who would never be forgotten.

Some Poems
by Robert Burns

TO A LOUSE,
ON SEEING ONE IN A LADY'S BONNET, AT CHURCH

Ha! whare ye gaun, ye crowlin ferlie!
Your impudence protects you sairly:
I canna say but ye strunt rarely
Owre gauze and lace;
Tho' faith! I fear, ye dine but sparely
On sic a place.

Ye ugly, creepin', blastit wonner,
Detested, shunn'd, by saunt an' sinner,
How dare ye set your fit upon her,
Sae fine a lady!
Gae somewhere else, and seek your dinner
On some poor body.

---

crowlin: crawling
ferlie: marvel
sairly: badly
strunt: strut
owre: over
sic: such
wonner: wonder
saunt: saint
fit: foot

Swith! in some beggar's hauffet squattle;
There ye may creep, and sprawl, and sprattle
Wi' ither kindred, jumping cattle,
In shoals and nations;
Whare horn nor bane ne'er daur unsettle
Your thick plantations.

Now haud you there, ye're out o' sight,
Below the fatt'rells, snug an' tight;
Na, faith ye yet! ye'll no be right
Till ye've got on it,
The vera topmost, tow'ring height
O' Miss's bonnet.

---

swith: quickly
hauffet: side of the head
squattle: squat
sprattle: scramble
bane: bone
daur: dare
haud: hold
fatt'rells: ribbon ends

My sooth! right bauld ye set your nose out,
As plump an' grey as onie grozet;
O for some rank, mercurial rozet,
Or fell, red smeddum,
I'd gie you sic a hearty doze o't,
Wad dross your droddum!

I wad na been suprpis'd to spy
You on an auld wife's flainen toy;
Or aiblins some bit duddie boy,
On's wyliecoat;
But Miss's fine Lunardi! fie!
How daur ye do't?

---

bauld: bold
onie: any
grozet: gooseberry
rank: abundant
rozet: resin
fell: strong
smeddum: spirit
dross: to crumble or crush
droddum: end or bottom
flainen: flannel
toy: an old fashioned headdress for ladies,
aiblins: perhaps
bit: small
duddie: ragged
wyliecoat: waistcoat
Lunardi: a type of very tall, balloon-

O, Jenny*, dinna toss your head,
An' set your beauties a' abroad!
Ye little ken what cursèd speed
The blastie's makin'!
Thae winks and finger-ends, I dread,
Are notice takin'!

O wad some Power the giftie gie us
To see oursels as ithers see us!
It wad frae monie a blunder free us
An' foolish notion;
What airs in dress an' gait wad lea'e us,
An' ev'n devotion!

---

shaped bonnet named after Vincent Lunardi, an
Italian noble who flew a hydrogen balloon in
Scotland in 1785
abread: abroad
thae: these
ithers: others
wa: would
frae: from
monie: many
lea'e: leave
*Jenny was a young woman from Mauchline.
Robbie wrote the poem after seeing a louse
crawling on her head and new bonnet when he
was in church.

ON SEEING A WOUNDED HARE LIMP BY ME, WHICH A FELLOW HAD JUST SHOT

Inhuman man! curse on thy barb'rous art,
And blasted be thy murder-aiming eye;
May never pity soothe thee with a sigh,
Nor ever pleasure glad thy cruel heart!

Go live, poor wanderer of the wood and field,
The bitter little of life that remains:
No more the thickening brakes and verdant plains
To thee shall home, or food, or pastime yield.

Seek, mangled wretch, some place of wonted rest,
No more of rest, but now thy dying bed!
The sheltering rushes whistling o'er thy head,
The cold earth with thy bloody bosom prest.

Oft as by winding Nith, I, musing, wait
The sober eve, or hail the cheerful dawn;
I'll miss thee sporting o'er the dewy lawn,
And curse the ruffian's aim, and mourn
                                    thy hapless fate.

---

verdant: grassy, green, fresh
Nith: the name of a river in the south west of
Scotland. Robert Burns later moved to a farm
beside the River Nith.

THE PLOUGHMAN

The ploughman he's a bonie lad,
His mind is ever true, jo,
His garters knit below his knee,
His bonnet it is blue, jo.

CHORUS
Then up wi't a' my ploughman lad,
And hey my merry ploughman!
Of a' the trades that I do ken,
Commend me to the ploughman.

My ploughman he comes hame at e'en,
He's aften wat and weary;
Cast off the wat, put on the dry,
And gae to bed, my dearie!

I will wash my ploughman's hose,
And I will dress his o'erlay;
I will mak my ploughman's bed,
And cheer him late and early.

---

jo: darling, sweetheart
ken: know
e'en: evening
aften: often
wat: wet
gae: go
hose: stockings
o'erlay: overlay

I hae been east, I hae been west,
I hae been at Saint Johnston;
The boniest sight that e'er I saw
Was the ploughman laddie dancin'.

Snaw-white stockins on his legs,
And siller buckles glancin';
A gude blue bonnet on his head,
And O, but he was handsome!

Commend me to the barn-yard,
And the corn-mou, man;
I never got my coggie fou,
Till I met wi' the ploughman.

Then up wi't a' my ploughman lad,
And hey my merry ploughman!
Of a' the trades that I do ken,
Commend me to the ploughman.

---

hae: have
e'er: ever
glancin': sparkling
gude: good
corn-mou: corn heap
gat: got
coggie: wooden dish
fou: full

A BARD'S EPITAPH*

Is there a whim-inspirèd fool,
Owre fast for thought, owre hot for rule,
Owre blate to seek, owre proud to snool?
Let him draw near;
And owre this grassy heap sing dool,
And drap a tear.

Is there a bard of rustic song,
Who, noteless, steals the crowds among,
That weekly this area throng?
O, pass not by!
But, with a frater-feeling strong,
Here, heave a sigh.

Is there a man, whose judgment clear
Can others teach the course to steer,
Yet runs, himself, life's mad career,
Wild as the wave?
Here pause – and, thro' the starting tear,
Survey this grave.

---

owre: over
blate: shy, bashful
snool: cringe
dool: sorrow
drap: drop
frater: brotherly

The poor inhabitant below
Was quick to learn and wise to know,
And keenly felt the friendly glow
And softer flame;
But thoughtless follies laid him low,
And stain'd his name!

Reader, attend! whether thy soul
Soars fancy's flights beyond the pole,
Or darkling grubs this earthly hole,
In low pursuit:
Know, prudent, cautious, self-control
Is wisdom's root.

---

*An epitaph is an inscription on a gravestone
which tells something about the person buried
there. Robert Burns wrote this epitaph about
himself. He knew that he was not perfect and
sometimes made mistakes but he always
meant well.

ADDRESS TO THE TOOTHACHE

My curse upon thy venom'd stang,
That shoots my tortur'd gooms alang;
And thro' my lug gies mony a twang,
Wi' gnawing vengeance,
Tearing my nerves wi' bitter pang,
Like racking engines!

When fevers burn, or ague freezes,
Rheumatics gnaw, or cholic squeezes,
Our neebors' sympathy may ease us,
Wi' pitying moan;
But thee – thou hell o' a' diseases,
Ay mocks our groan!

---

stang: sting,
gooms: gums
twang: twinge
alang: along
lug: ear
pang: ache, pain
racking: rocking, jarring
ague: a sickness, illness
cholic: stomach pains, wind
neebors: neighbours
ay: always

Adown my beard the slavers trickle!
I kick the wee stools o'er the mickle,
As round the fire the giglets keckle,
To see me loup;
An' raving mad, I wish a heckle
Were i' their doup.

O' a' the num'rous human dools,
Ill-har'sts, daft bargains, cutty-stools,
Or worthy frien's rak'd i' the mools,
Sad sight to see!
The tricks o' knaves, or fash o' fools –
Thou bears't the gree.

---

giglets: giggling youngsters or maidens,
keckle: cackle, cluck,
loup: leap
heckle: a sharp comb, sharp instrument,
doup: bottom
dools: woes , calamities, troubles
ill-har'sts: bad harvests
cutty-stools were short, three-legged stools
used in Scottish churches. A person being
shamed in public for some misbehaviour
had to stand on the cutty-stool in church
where everyone could see them
rak'd in the mools: buried in the crumbling
earth or grave
fash: trouble, annoyance
bears't the gree: win the victory, hold first
place

Whare'er that place be priests ca' Hell,
Whare a' the tones o' mis'ry yell,
An' rankèd plagues their numbers tell,
In dreadfu' raw,
Thou, Toothache, surely bear'st the bell
Amang them a'!

O thou grim, mischief-making chiel,
That gars the notes of discord squeel,
Till daft mankind aft dance a reel
In gore' a shoe-thick!
Gie' a' the faes o' Scotland's weal
A towmond's toothache.

---

raw: row
chiel: fellow,
gars: causes, makes,
faes: foes, enemies,
weal: well,
a towmond's toothache: a twelve month
    toothache

CA' THE YOWES TO THE KNOWES

CHORUS:
Ca' the yowes to the knowes
Ca' them whare the heather grows
Ca' them whare the burnie rowes
    My bonie dearie!

As I gaed down the water-side,
There I met my shepherd lad:
He row'd me sweetly in his plaid.
    And he ca'd me his dearie.

'Will ye gang down the water-side.
And see the waves sae sweetly glide
Beneath the hazels spreading wide,
    The Moon it shines fu' clearly?'

'I was bred up in nae sic school,
My shepherd lad, to play the fool,
An' a' the day to sit in dool,
    An' naebody to see me.'

---

ca': drive
yowe: ewe (female sheep)
knowes: knolls, hills
dool: sorrow

'Ye sall get gowns and ribbons meet,
Cauf-leather shoon upon your feet,
And in my arms ye'se lie an sleep,
   And' ye sall be my dearie.'

'If ye'll but stand to what ye've said,
I'se gang wi' you, my shepherd lad,
And ye may row me in your plaid
   And I sall be your dearie.'

'While waters wimple to the see,
While day blinks the lift sae hie,
Till clay-cauld death sall blin' my e'e
   Ye sall be may dearie.'

---

wimple: wind
blinks: shines

WILLIE BREW'D A PECK O' MAUT

CHORUS:
We are na fou, we're nae that fou
*   But just a drappie on our e'e!*
The cock may craw, the day may daw,
*   An ay we'll taste the barley bree!*

Oh, Willie brewed a peck o' maut,
    And Rob and Allan cam to prie.
Three blyther hearts that lee-lang night
    Ye wad na found in Christendie.

Here are we met three merry boys,
    Three merry boys I trow are we;
And monie a night we've merry been,
    And monie mae we hope to be.

It is the moon, I ken her horn,
    That's blinkin in the lift sae hie;
She shines sae bright to wyle us hame,
    But, by my sooth, she'll wait a wee!

Wha first sall rise to gang awa,
    A cuckold, coward loun is he!
Wha first beside his chair shall fa',
    He is the King amang us three!

---

maut: malt
fou: full (i.e. drunk)

THE SLAVE'S LAMENT

It was in sweet Senegal
That my foes did me enthral
   For the lands of Virginia, -ginia, O!
Torn from that lovely shore,
And must never see it more,
   And alas! I am weary, weary, O!

All on that charming coast
Is no bitter snow and frost,
   Like the lands of Virginia, -ginia, O!
There streams for ever flow,
And the flowers for ever blow,
   And alas! I am weary, weary, O!

The burden I must bear,
While the cruel scourge I fear,
   In the lands of Virginia, -ginia, O!
And I think on friends most dear
With the bitter, bitter tear,
   And alas! I am weary, weary, O!

AULD LANG SYNE

Should auld acquaintance be forgot,
And never brought to mind?
Should auld acquaintance be forgot,
And auld lang syne?

CHORUS
For auld lang syne, my jo,
For auld lang syne,
We'll tak a cup o' kindness yet,
For auld lang syne!

And surely ye'll be your pint-stowp,
And surely I'll be mine;
And we'll tak a cup o' kindness yet,
For auld lang syne.

We twa hae run about the braes,
And pu't the gowans fine;
But we've wander'd mony a weary foot,
Sin' auld lang syne.

---

min': mind, remembrance
lang syne: long ago
pint-stowp: pint tankard
twa: two
hae: have
braes: hills
pu't: pulled
gowans: daisies
mony: many
sin': since

121

We twa hae paidl't i' the burn,
Frae mornin' sun till dine;
But seas between us braid hae roar'd,
Sin' auld lang syne.

And there's a hand, my trusty fiere,
And gie's a hand o' thine;
And we'll tak a right guid-willie waught,
For auld lang syne.

For auld lang syne, my dear,
For auld lang syne,
We'll tak a cup o' kindness yet,
For auld lang syne!

---

paidl't: paddled
burn: stream
frae: from
dine: dinner time
braid: broad
fiere: friend, comrade
gie's: give us
guid-willie waught: merry draught, drink

Robert Burns (1759–1796)
BIOGRAPHICAL FACTS

1786 The Kilmarnock *Poems* published
Twin babies are born to Jean Armour
Burns arrives in Edinburgh

1787 Grand Lodge of Scotland toasts Burns as
'Caledonia's Bard'
Edinburgh *Poems* published
Burns returns to Mauchline and sets up
home with Jean Armour

1788 Burns becomes an Excise man

1790 Volume III of *Scots Musical Museum*
published
Burns transferred to Dumfries

1793 *Tam o' Shanter* first published
Second edition of Edinburgh *Poems*
published

1795 Burns ill with rheumatic fever

1796 Burns dies

FURTHER INFORMATION

www.gla.ac.uk/robertburnsstudies/

www.robertburns.org/works/

www.bbc.co.uk/robertburns/

www.nls.uk/burns/

www.burnsheritagepark.com/

www.robertburns.org.uk/

www.worldburnsclub.com/

www.electricscotland.com/burns/